AUSTRALIA

Alexis Roumanis

LET'S READ

AV²
BY WEIGL™

ADDED VALUE • AUDIO VISUAL

Go to **www.av2books.com**, and enter this book's unique code.

BOOK CODE

J442678

AV² by Weigl brings you media enhanced books that support active learning.

AV² provides enriched content that supplements and complements this book. Weigl's AV² books strive to create inspired learning and engage young minds in a total learning experience.

Your AV² Media Enhanced books come alive with...

Audio
Listen to sections of the book read aloud.

Video
Watch informative video clips.

Embedded Weblinks
Gain additional information for research.

Try This!
Complete activities and hands-on experiments.

Key Words
Study vocabulary, and complete a matching word activity.

Quizzes
Test your knowledge.

Slide Show
View images and captions, and prepare a presentation.

... and much, much more!

Published by AV² by Weigl
350 5th Avenue, 59th Floor New York, NY 10118
Websites: www.av2books.com   www.weigl.com

Library of Congress Cataloging-in-Publication Data

Roumanis, Alexis.
 Australia / Alexis Roumanis.
    pages cm. -- (Exploring continents)
 Includes index.
 ISBN 978-1-4896-3034-6 (hard cover : alk. paper) -- ISBN 978-1-4896-3035-3 (soft cover : alk. paper) --
 ISBN 978-1-4896-3036-0 (single user ebook) -- ISBN 978-1-4896-3037-7 (multi-user ebook)
 1. Australia--Juvenile literature. I. Title.
 DU96.R68 2014
 994--dc23
                                                 2014044125
Printed in the United States of America in Brainerd, Minnesota
1 2 3 4 5 6 7 8 9 0 18 17 16 15 14

122014   Project Coordinator: Jared Siemens
WEP051214   Design: Mandy Christiansen

Weigl acknowledges iStock and Getty Images as the primary image suppliers for this title.

AUSTRALIA

Contents

**Welcome to Australia.
It is the smallest continent.**

6

This is the shape
of Australia.
Asia lies to the
north of Australia.
Antarctica sits
to the south.

Where Is Australia?

Two oceans touch
the coast of Australia.

Australia is made up of many different landforms. Deserts, mountains, plains, and rainforests can all be found in Australia.

The Great Victoria Desert is the largest desert in Australia.

Lake Eyre is the largest salt lake in Australia.

Wallaman Falls is the tallest waterfall in Australia.

Mount Kosciuszko is the tallest mountain in Australia.

The Murray River is the longest river in Australia.

Koalas can sleep as much as 20 hours each day.

Kangaroos can jump up to 10 feet (3 meters) high.

The echidna is one of only two mammals in the world that lay eggs.

Australia is home to some of the world's most unique animals. Many different kinds of animals live there.

The scrub python is the largest snake in Australia.

The emu is the largest bird in Australia.

Australia is home to many different types of plants.

The Huon pine can live for more than 3,000 years.

The mountain ash is the tallest kind of tree in Australia.

Macadamia trees can grow up to 50 pounds (23 kilograms) of nuts each year.

The golden wattle is Australia's national flower.

Banksia flowers are sometimes called giant candles.

Australia's only country has the same name as the continent. It is more than 100 years old. People have lived in Australia for thousands of years.

Aboriginal Australians are one of the first peoples of Australia.

Many kinds of people live in Australia. Each group of people is special in its own way.

Some Aboriginals wear body paint for important events.

A didjeridu is an instrument played by Aboriginal Austalians.

A boomerang can be used to hunt animals.

Dancing is an important part of Aboriginal life.

More than 23 million people live in Australia. There are six states in Australia.

The city with the most people in Australia is Sydney.

There are many things that can be found only in Australia.
People come from all over the world to visit this continent.

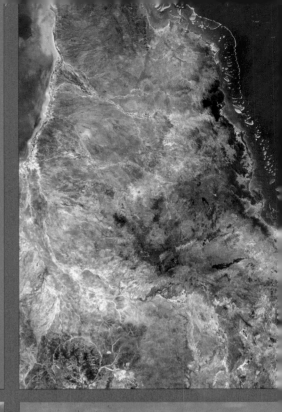

The color of Uluru changes during the day.

Fraser Island is the largest sand island in the world.

The Great Barrier Reef is so large it can be seen from space.

Parts of the Sydney Opera House were made to look like boat sails.

The Bungle Bungle Range has large striped rocks shaped like beehives.

Australia Quiz

See what you have learned
about the continent
of Australia.

What do these pictures tell you
about Australia?

KEY WORDS BEA PIC R

Research has shown that as much as 65 percent of all written material published in English is made up of 300 words. These 300 words cannot be taught using pictures or learned by sounding them out. They must be recognized by sight. This book contains 78 common sight words to help young readers improve their reading fluency and comprehension. This book also teaches young readers several important content words, such as proper nouns. These words are paired with pictures to aid in learning and improve understanding.

Page	Sight Words First Appearance
4	is, it, the, to
7	of, this, two, where
8	all, and, be, can, different, found, great, in, made, many, mountains, up
9	river
10	as, day, each, feet, high, much, one, only, that, world
11	animals, home, kinds, live, most, some, there
12	for, grow, more, plants, than, tree, years
13	are, sometimes
15	country, first, has, have, name, old, people, same
16	an, by, group, important, its, own, way
17	life, part
19	city, states, with
20	changes, come, from, large, over, so, things
21	house, like, look, were

Page	Content Words First Appearance
4	Australia, continent
7	Antarctica, Asia, coast, oceans, shape
8	deserts, lake, landforms, plains, rainforests, waterfall
10	echidna, eggs, kangaroos, koalas, mammals
11	bird, emu, scrub python, snake
12	nuts, pine
13	flower, candles
15	Aboriginal
16	instrument, paint
17	boomerang, dancing
19	Sydney
20	sand, space
21	beehives, rocks, sails

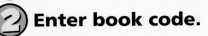